Limited Government

Sujith Vijay

ISBN-13: 979-8846683488

Cover image: *Washington Crossing the Delaware* by Emanuel Leutze.

Dedicated to the loving memory of my brother Renjith Vijay (1985 - 2015)

CONTENTS

Chapter 1: Origins of Government

On 28th March 1977, Peter Finch became the first posthumous Oscar winner in the Best Actor category for his portrayal of the charismatic and rather unhinged television anchor Howard Beale in the movie *Network*. There are many memorable scenes and dialogues in this movie, but none as timeless as Beale's rant on live television that captures the disaffection and frustration of the public with their government.

I don't have to tell you things are bad. Everybody knows things are bad. It's a depression. Everybody's out of work or scared of losing their job. The dollar buys a nickel's worth; banks are going bust; shopkeepers keep a gun under the counter; punks are running wild in the street, and there's nobody anywhere who seems to know what to do, and there's no end to it. We know the air is unfit to breathe and our food is unfit to eat. ... We sit in the house, and slowly the world we're living in is getting smaller, and all we say is, "Please, at least leave us alone in our living rooms. Let me have my toaster and my TV and my steel-belted radials, and I won't say anything. Just leave us alone."

Well, I'm not going to leave you alone. I want you to get mad! ... I don't know what to do about the depression and the inflation and the Russians and the crime in the street. All I know is that first, you've got to get mad. You've gotta say, "I'm a human being, goddammit! My life has value!" So, I want you to get up now. I want all of you to get up out of your chairs. I want you to get up right now and go to the window, open it, and stick your head out and yell, "I'm as mad as hell, and I'm not going to take this anymore!"

The clarion call is taken up by viewers all over the country, providing a much-needed boost to the sagging ratings of Beale's show. But the broader message of his spiel is that any government that takes its citizens for granted does so at its peril. Society is all about positive-sum games that enhance cooperation among individuals and making a whole that exceeds the sum of its parts. Governments become necessary as a regulatory mechanism to ensure that this goal is not sabotaged by an individual or an organisation. The challenge for governments is to implement this mandate without getting drunk on power or trampling on the rights of the governed.

Governments in the modern era can be broadly subdivided into two categories, namely monarchies and republics. Monarchies evolved out of tribal chiefdoms and were the dominant form of government pretty much everywhere in the world, until a few centuries ago. (Notable exceptions in this regard were Athens, Carthage and Rome.) Many monarchs asserted that their right to rule and reign was of divine origin. For example, it took a catastrophic defeat and nuclear bombardment for Emperor Hirohito of Japan to publicly renounce his divinity on New Year's Day, 1946.

In contrast, republics have always been ruled by representatives elected from among the citizens. Although voting rights were restricted in the past based on gender, race, land ownership and education, the ruling class was more accountable to the people in the republican system of government, compared to monarchies. Today, only about a fifth of the sovereign nations of the world are monarchies, while the rest are republics. Moreover, in many of these monarchies, including the United Kingdom, the role of the monarch is largely ceremonial. (The last British monarch to dismiss a Prime Minister was King William IV in 1834.)

Ultimately, accepting any form of government entails the sacrifice of individual freedom to some extent. When a large number of people deal with entities and systems in which they have some sort of stake, yet not exactly ownership, mere appeal to good manners is often insufficient and laws become necessary. Forests, roads, rivers and groundwater benefit everyone, but nobody should be allowed to take undue advantage of them. Governments arise out of the need to balance individual freedom with social stability. As the French philosopher Simone Weil noted, *"The notion of obligations comes before that of rights, which is subordinate and relative to the former. A right is not effectual by itself, but only in relation to the obligation to which it corresponds."*

In particular, citizens can enjoy only those rights that those in power are prepared to concede. A despotic ruler with an intent to cement his legacy through military conquests and ostentatious monuments has no incentive to open the coffers of the treasury for the welfare of the people. The earliest challenge to this state of affairs, at least in the Western world, was the revolt of the feudal barons against King John of England, resulting in the signing of the first draft of the *Magna Carta* in 1215. This declaration ensured that the King's authority on taxation and incarceration was not limitless, but guided by established principles enshrining justice and the rule of law. This was the beginning of the end for the notions of divine origins of monarchy, not just in England, but everywhere in Europe.

Chapter 2: Hobbes and Locke

Four centuries after King John signed the Magna Carta, civil war broke out in England between the *Roundheads* led by Sir Thomas Fairfax and Oliver Cromwell, and the *Cavaliers* who sympathised with King Charles I. The Roundheads sought to establish the sovereignty of the parliament, transforming England from an absolute monarchy to a constitutional monarchy. Charles I was captured, tried and executed in 1649, leading to a short-lived political entity known as the Commonwealth of England headed by Cromwell. The commonwealth fizzled out after Cromwell's death in 1658, and monarchy was restored in

1660 when Charles II, the eldest surviving son of Charles I, returned from exile.

Right in the middle of all this mess, in 1651, English political philosopher Thomas Hobbes published a treatise titled *Leviathan* (named after a sea serpent mentioned several times in the Old Testament) in defence of absolute monarchy. Hobbes expounded on human nature, society and the legitimacy of governments. He noted at the outset that in the absence of social order and an authority to enforce laws, life would be *"solitary, poor, nasty, brutish and short"*. Hobbes had a rather dim view of human nature, arguing that aggregate goodness was bounded due to the inherent variability of human desires, while aggregate evil was essentially unbounded due to the universal fear of violent death. Therefore, the state should be organised around prevention of evil rather than the pursuit of the good, as this was the only way to foster the cooperation of citizens.

Implicit in the arguments of *Leviathan* was that a rebellion against the government should be avoided at all costs. While it is true that all governments will have to take difficult decisions from time to time that alienate some of their constituents, it is also not uncommon that people in power, through malice or idiocy, make living conditions far worse than they would have been with sensible management. Just as falsifiability by experiment is a strength of modern science rather than a weakness, the possibility of regime change by revolution should really strengthen the government by aligning its interests with those of the citizens. Thus argued English philosopher John Locke in a series of works culminating in the *Two Treatises of Government*, anonymously published in 1689, around the same time as the bloodless Glorious Revolution saw the ascent of King William III and his wife Queen Mary II as joint rulers, overthrowing King James II. Indeed, Locke served as an advisor to King

William and Queen Mary, and was the major architect of the *English Bill of Rights*, signed into law by the King and Queen in 1689. The Bill of Rights would go on to have a significant influence on the eventual development of the constitution of the United States, and Locke is universally revered as the father of modern liberalism.

Both Hobbes and Locke spoke of a **social contract** that the citizens engage in, though the term itself was coined only in 1762, by Genevan philosopher Jean Jacques Rousseau. Hobbes thought of the social contract as an agreement among the people whereby certain freedoms were voluntarily conceded in exchange for the security and social order that a powerful sovereign, usually a monarch, would provide. Locke, on the other hand, thought of the social contract as not just existing among the people, but between the people and the rulers as well. The **consent of the governed** is the source of legitimacy of the government. There is not so much a concession of one person's liberty as a recognition of the other person's liberty as well. The principal role of the government is akin to that of a magistrate rather than that of a police officer, since no man can be an impartial judge in his own cause. Locke also believed, in contrast to Hobbes, that human nature was guided by tolerance and reason.

So who is right? Locke's optimism may have won the battle in political science departments of universities throughout the world, but in the trenches of *realpolitik*, Hobbes continues to be a formidable adversary. Over the last ten years or so, the portrait of the Premier as a strongman has been gaining currency all over the world, and civil liberties are often endangered as a result. The real solution may be to encourage and elect governments that would gradually nudge human nature closer to Locke's view compared to Hobbes's view, rather than close our eyes and pretend that evil does not exist. As Martin Luther King Jr. said, *"The arc of the moral universe is long, but it bends towards justice. Change takes a long time, but it does happen."*

Chapter 3: The American Revolution

In January 1776, as a storm of dissatisfaction and dissent was brewing across the thirteen British colonies that would evolve over centuries into the present-day United States, an anonymous 47-page pamphlet titled *Common Sense* gained popularity among the revolutionaries. The author turned out to be an Englishman named Thomas Paine who had landed on the American continent only in 1774. The pamphlet sold more than 100,000 copies within three months of its publication, at a time when the combined population of the colonies was only around two million. Paine is widely credited as energising the masses with the zeal of the revolution that had hitherto remained within rebel hideouts and secret tavern meetings.

Common Sense was a blistering attack against the institution of monarchy in general and the practice of hereditary succession in particular. Paine's unsparing prose demolished the purported divine origins of kings and questioned the legitimacy of the British Crown. He argued that American revolutionaries should not merely declare independence, but establish a new kind of government based on representation and equality. The following excerpt is indicative of his tone and tenor:

"England since the conquest hath known some few good monarchs, but groaned beneath a much larger number of bad ones: yet no man in his senses can say that their claim under William the Conqueror is a very honourable one. A French bastard landing with an armed Banditti and establishing himself king of England against the consent of the natives, is in plain terms a very paltry rascally original. It certainly hath no divinity in it. However, it is needless to spend much time in exposing the folly of hereditary right; if there are any so weak as to believe it, let them promiscuously worship the Ass and

the Lion, and welcome. I shall neither copy their humility, nor disturb their devotion."

Although *Common Sense* was quite popular with the masses, Paine's ideas and rhetoric were considered rather incendiary, even by the leaders of the American revolution. Thus, when Thomas Jefferson drafted the Declaration of Independence later that year, he modelled it more on John Locke's *Two Treatises of Government* rather than on Paine's vision. As we saw, Locke was no docile pacifist himself, and the Declaration's famous line, *"whenever any form of government becomes destructive of these ends, it is the right of the people to alter or to abolish it, and to institute new government"*, is clearly influenced by Locke. Sadly, many of Paine's ideas were far ahead of his time, such as an unsuccessful negotiation in his later years to abolish slavery in the newly acquired territory of Louisiana. Only six people attended the funeral of this great man when he died in 1809, mainly because of his disdain for organised religion.

The American revolutionary war ended in 1783, when the representatives of King George III signed the Treaty of Paris, officially recognising the independence and sovereignty of the United States. But it took several years before the thirteen colonies could agree on a constitution for the new nation. A principal sticking point was the absence of a Bill of Rights similar to the one passed in England a century earlier. The Federalists led by Alexander Hamilton and James Madison believed that the constitution as it stood, with its doctrine of separation of governmental powers into the legislative, executive and judicial branches, was adequately equipped to ensure civil liberties of the people, while Anti-Federalists like Patrick Henry, Samuel Adams and John Hancock thought that the constitution as written would lead to too much concentration of power in the hands of the federal government and a dictatorship remained possible. In the end, the Federalists prevailed and the constitution was ratified, somewhat grudgingly. But by then James Madison, the principal architect of the United States constitution, had come to appreciate the reasoning of his rivals and proposed ten amendments to the constitution, and together these became the *United States Bill of Rights*. These amendments, ratified in 1791, included the freedom of speech and expression, the right to keep and bear arms, protection against unreasonable searches and seizures, right against self-incrimination and the right to a fair trial by jury, among others.

The principal difference between the English and the American versions of the Bill of Rights was that the former sought to protect citizens against royal high-handedness by giving more power to the elected representatives of the parliament, while the latter sought to protect citizens against governmental overreach at all levels by ensuring civil liberties for the individual. Not all of these liberties are readily apparent; for example, the Second Amendment allowing private citizens to bear arms has been at the centre of the gun control debate in the United States that continues to this day. However, a constitution that acknowledges the fallibility of elected representatives is less likely to slip into a totalitarian regime than one that confuses an election mandate with a *carte blanche* to rule with abandon. In times of war or financial distress, people will appreciate the efficiency of a strong ruler, and the erosion of individual and minority freedoms will be viewed as bitter medicine to secure peace and harmony. After all, one does not realise that the right to protest against the government has been taken away until there is something to protest about. Only by enshrining human rights in the constitution as non-negotiable freedoms can such unpleasant developments be nipped in the bud.

Chapter 4: Free Speech

Shortly after the United States made a delayed entry into the First World War, socialists Charles Schenk and Elizabeth Baer were arrested for the offence of undermining the American military by printing and distributing pamphlets to citizens, encouraging them to resist conscription. The defendants argued that they were merely exercising their freedom of speech, but the Supreme Court unanimously upheld the conviction. *"The most stringent protection of free speech would not protect a man in falsely shouting fire in a theatre and causing a panic"*, wrote Justice Oliver Wendell Holmes in the judgement of Schenck v.

United States (1919). Subsequent legal scholars have questioned the appropriateness of this analogy, but it remains deeply rooted in the public psyche as an illustration that not all speech can be protected by law. As for the judgement itself, though Holmes drew the line for restricting speech at a *"clear and present danger"* that the words used could bring about evils that the laws of the land are designed to prevent, it was mollified by the Supreme Court five decades later in Brandenburg v. Ohio (1969) to apply only to cases where there was incitement of *"imminent lawless action".*

Not all nations have taken such a liberal view of the matter. There are countries like the Philippines where truth alone is not a defence against defamation; one must also demonstrate that public interest is served by the publication of unpleasant truths that can cause damage to someone's reputation. Although there have not been any prosecutions till date, it is a criminal offence in Canada to refer to a person by their biologically apparent pronoun if it is different from their preferred personal pronoun. Many theocracies have laws that not merely convict, but impose capital punishment for blasphemy.

But such laws do not directly impede the right of citizens to criticise their government, except as instruments at the disposal of governments to incarcerate their critics by poring over past statements and interviews. In a perfect world, governments will value criticism more than sycophancy, as constructive criticism invariably brings to their attention how some of their well-intentioned policies fail to deliver where the rubber meets the road. We don't live anywhere close to a perfect world; we live in one where tin-pot movie dictators from Rufus T. Firefly to Admiral General Aladeen bear uncanny resemblance to powerful rulers of our time, many of whom are democratically elected.

Before the advent of social media, free speech essentially meant freedom of the press and broadcasting networks. The government knew whom to keep tabs on, and how to use print and visual media as tools of propaganda. Until a few decades ago, radio stations and television channels were exclusively state-owned in many countries. Even today, an unholy nexus between governments and corporations often ensures that the mass media market remains an oligopoly.

But then the internet came along, and changed the rules of the game. Information started flowing more freely, and along with it, inconvenient truths. Whistleblowers began to aim directly at the public, eliminating the gatekeepers and the middlemen. Even state secrets were out in the open, thanks to the work of Julian Assange and Edward Snowden, among others.

The case for free speech is no longer clear in some of these contexts. Without discussing the merit of individual cases, not least because many of the well-known instances are still *sub judice*, the heart of the matter is the need to keep strategic secrets from falling into the hands of malicious actors like terrorist organisations, or even foreign governments. National security is the top priority of any government, and free expression doesn't stand a chance if allowing it would make the nation more vulnerable to external aggression, civil war or a bank run. (Of course, such objections have to be backed by evidence that would hold up in court.) However, the situation is different when the legislature passes a law empowering the government to pursue a certain course of action, and the executive branch clandestinely oversteps the limits of the law because the public would never agree if they were told the whole truth. Whistleblowers who bring such abuses of power to light would be acting more democratically than the government officials themselves.

Another grey area is about the restrictions on free speech that private companies can impose. Social media companies restrict the visibility of user-generated content for various reasons, and users could also be banned outright. Sometimes this could be under the pretext of fact-checking, although the underlying science may be far from settled. Allegations of bullying or offensive behaviour could also be involved, yet the line between a harsh comment and a nasty insult is often blurred by moral outrage. Inadequate fail-safe mechanisms like a threshold of negative reports before action is taken are easily bypassed via mass reporting. The law generally does not offer much by way of protection to social media users in most of these cases, as the data servers are not maintained with taxpayer money. On the other hand, deplatforming an electoral candidate in the middle of a campaign is certainly a matter of public interest. One can only hope that laws will eventually evolve and adapt to such scenarios as they have done in the past, especially when dealing with large corporations that have a corner on the digital outreach market.

Chapter 5: Central Planning

In 1991, faced with a crippling balance of payment crisis triggered by the collapse of long-standing ally Soviet Union and a spike in oil prices brought about by the Gulf War, the Indian government approached the World Bank and the International Monetary Fund for financial assistance. India ended up receiving substantial aid, but only after the government agreed to open up the economy for foreign investment in many sectors that had been the monopoly of state-owned enterprises. This marked the beginning of India's transition from a Soviet-style centrally planned economy to a mixed economy, incorporating many features of the market economies of North America and Western Europe, while also retaining state-ownership and price controls in certain essential sectors. In spite of considerable domestic criticism and cries of betrayal at the time, these reforms are now widely recognised as lifting millions out of poverty and considerably improving the standard of living of Indian citizens.

Indeed, the worldwide contest between central planning and market economy is now done and dusted. With the possible exception of North Korea, no government in the present day can get away with fixing prices or imposing production quotas unless there is a national emergency. Prices are decided by the law of supply and demand, and what Adam Smith called the *"invisible hand of the market"* has invariably achieved better economic growth and prosperity in the medium to long term than a council of experts with the best of intentions. The World Trade Organisation has 164 member nations, accounting for 98% of the global GDP, who have agreed to use subsidies, tariffs and other protectionist measures only sparingly and in accordance with internationally agreed principles.

But why did so many countries give up on central planning? It simply turned out to be an inefficient way of allocating resources. In September 1945, libertarian economist Friedrich Hayek published an article titled *The Use of Knowledge in Society* in the academic journal *The American Economic Review*. Hayek outlined how most of the relevant information for making correct aggregate decisions at the governmental level lie in specific constraints of individual households and small businesses that will never be known to any central authority, but is embedded in the price information of goods and services. This disconnect with reality, he argued, was why centrally planned economies would underperform market economies. Hayek wrote,

"One reason why economists are increasingly apt to forget about the constant small changes which make up the whole economic picture is probably their growing preoccupation with statistical aggregates, which show a very much greater stability than the movements of the detail. The comparative stability of the aggregates cannot, however, be accounted for—as the statisticians occasionally seem to be inclined to do—by the 'law of large numbers' or the mutual compensation of random changes. The number of elements with which we have to deal is not large enough for such accidental forces to produce stability. ... The statistics which such a central authority would have to use would have to be arrived

at precisely by abstracting from minor differences between the things, by lumping together, as resources of one kind, items which differ as regards location, quality, and other particulars, in a way which may be very significant for the specific decision. It follows from this that central planning based on statistical information by its nature cannot take direct account of these circumstances of time and place and that the central planner will have to find some way or other in which the decisions depending on them can be left to the 'man on the spot.' "

International developments in subsequent decades vindicated Hayek's position, as even former socialist nations embraced principles of the free market. However, an absolute market economy exists only in textbooks. If nothing else, there needs to be enough governmental control to ensure an environment that allows fair competition in the marketplace, to restrict monopolies and cartels, and to ensure the delivery of essential goods and services like consumer staples, healthcare and electricity. Even the United States, dubbed the *"last bastion of capitalism"* by Vladimir Lenin, could not escape price controls during the Second World War. When President Harry Truman ended these measures in June 1946, ignoring the advice of several distinguished economists who urged an extension for one more year, he saw inflation skyrocket from an annualised rate of 3.3% to 18.1% in just six months. The disgruntled electorate handed Truman and the Democratic Party a stinging defeat in the midterm elections later that year, with the Republican Party controlling both houses of Congress for the first time since 1928. The people had spoken.

But even if there is a case for governmental intervention in certain climates and circumstances, there is usually considerable pushback when that happens. Obesity may be a public health issue, but nobody likes to be told what to eat by bureaucrats from the health department. Automobiles may contribute to environmental pollution and climate change, but mandating the use of mass transit, especially if it results in a much longer daily commute, may not sit well with the public. The pejorative term 'nanny state', introduced by British conservative politician Iain Macleod, is an apposite metaphor for governments that unduly interfere in the daily lives of individuals.

Yet the line between due and undue interference is not always clear. During the COVID-19 pandemic, most governments made vaccination mandatory for all adults, but booster doses were deemed optional. One can posit an implicit price of individual liberty based on data points such as these. Just as governments have a mandate to ensure a floor as well as a ceiling on food prices to support both farmers and consumers, they also have the mandate of pricing liberty in harmony with both individual agency and collective welfare.

Chapter 6: The Welfare State

The role of governments in safeguarding the life and property of citizens is well understood. However, this is not merely a law and order issue. Loss of wealth can happen not just by natural disasters or looting, but also by imprudent management of public finances by federal and local governments. For example, poor economic policies can result in runaway inflation, eroding the value of the currency and diminishing the purchasing power of citizens. Often, unsustainable welfare schemes designed to propitiate the electorate and garner votes push the next generation of citizens, none of whom are old enough to vote and some of whom are yet to draw breath, under a mountain of public debt. Austerity measures and capital controls would soon follow, and the standards of living would drop drastically.

By then, the government that caused all the mischief would likely be sitting in the opposition benches and criticising their hapless successors for abandoning the populist sops that led to the mess in the first place. Plenty of irony and not a tinge of remorse. In other words, politics as usual.

The welfare state is, without doubt, the crowning achievement of modern society. Disability pensions, unemployment benefits and universal healthcare go a long way towards taking the sting out of the quills that life tends to shoot at all and sundry. However, there is only so much welfare a country can afford without bankrupting itself. The threshold value for the sustainable ratio of public debt to gross domestic product depends on clout and country, but anything above 90% is usually asking for trouble. With apologies to the screenwriters of the movie *Top Gun*, the heart should not be writing checks the hand can't cash.

Belgian economist André Sapir has come up with a classification of European welfare states into four categories, namely Nordic (Sweden, Finland, Norway, Denmark and the

Netherlands), Anglo-Saxon (United Kingdom and Ireland), Continental (Austria, Belgium, France, Germany and Luxembourg) and Mediterranean (Greece, Italy, Portugal and Spain). After a thorough analysis of these models, he concludes that the Nordic system achieves both efficiency (maximum employment) and equity (minimum poverty), while the Mediterranean system accomplishes neither. The Continental and Anglo-Saxon systems have to choose between the two goals, with the former obtaining efficiency at the expense of equity, and the latter obtaining the opposite. It is worth noting that the Nordic model is highly deregulated while the Mediterranean model is heavily interventionist, perhaps partially accounting for the disparities in their success.

However, the Nordic model is not something a low or middle income country can adapt overnight. To begin with, the highest tax rate is close to 60% in Sweden and Denmark, and the other countries are not too far behind. While the citizens enjoy universal healthcare, free college tuition and subsidised public transport, not everything is free. Ultimately, these countries can afford to have such high tax rates only because the per capita national income, and by extension, the average salary, is also high. Of course, free access to education and healthcare also means that the society is far more egalitarian than most other countries, so the median income, or even the tenth percentile income, for that matter, is high as well. All this works out because these countries never had a Malthusian disadvantage of high population and low resources, and were quite well off to begin with.

However, in the age of open borders and unrestricted immigration, the Nordic model appears to be under threat. Sweden had the highest influx of asylum seekers when adjusted for population, among all European countries in 2015, at the height of the Syrian crisis. Large scale immigration of unskilled workers has widened income inequality, increased the violent crime rate and stretched the funding for the social safety net. When the Swedish government boldly decided to abandon lockdowns in favour of self-restraint of citizens during the COVID-19 pandemic, it was a red-letter day for civil liberties and participatory democracy. However, subsequent studies showed that immigrant-dense areas were most severely affected by the virus, partly due to government communications and expert advice being inaccessible to most of the immigrant population, due to their lack of proficiency in Swedish. In the end, the real flaw in the Swedish strategy was the fallibility of herd immunity assumptions rather than a sociological miscalculation, but one wonders how things might have turned out had this pandemic hit the world a decade earlier than it did, when Sweden had a more linguistically homogeneous population than it does now.

Chapter 7: Mass Surveillance

In the aftermath of the September 11 terrorist attacks in 2001, the United States Congress enacted the Patriot Act to provide the government with appropriate tools to restrict, intercept and obstruct terrorism. Although the act contained many sunset provisions to limit its applicability beyond 2005, the essential powers granted to the government were renewed in some shape or form, all the way until 2019. Several provisions of this act were, according to many legal scholars, in clear contravention of the US Bill of Rights, especially the Fourth Amendment that granted citizens protection from unreasonable searches and wiretaps without probable cause. The Patriot Act also allowed the indefinite detention of immigrants without trial. Clearly, if such a measure is helpful in deterring terrorism, it should apply to citizens as well, so it seems reasonable to surmise that such a measure, if applied to citizens, would be unconstitutional. In other words, the nation of immigrants, the sweet land of liberty, openly introduced a parallel legal system for immigrants with fewer civil rights — all in the name of safety.

But don't terrorists have the advantage of surprise, and shouldn't governments be able to prevent attacks by any means necessary, social costs be damned? Unfortunately, measures ostensibly meant to freeze terrorists in their tracks often achieve nothing of the sort; they only help in concentrating power in the hands of law enforcement officials and various government agencies. Routine surveillance of political rivals gives an unfair advantage for the incumbent political party in elections, and the dilution of due process provides ample opportunities to incarcerate critics, gadflies and intransigent intellectuals. Targeted surveillance is indispensable for public safety; mass surveillance inevitably leads to a police state.

In the absence of terrorist attacks, a war would provide the same pretext. Nothing guarantees re-election like an ongoing war. Elbert Hubbard, in his collection of biographical essays titled *Little Journeys to the Homes of the Great*, describes how a military conflict is often the best thing that could happen to a struggling government.

"The army is used for two purposes — to coerce disturbers at home, and to get up a war at a distance, and thus distract attention from the troubles near at hand. Napoleon used to say that the only sure cure for internal dissension was a foreign war: this would draw the disturbers away, on the plea of patriotism, so they would win enough outside loot to satisfy them, or else they would all get killed, it really didn't matter much; and as for loot, if

it was taken from foreigners, there was no sin."

Of course, mass surveillance is a lot easier in totalitarian states like China. In 2014, the Chinese government launched a social credit system, combining facial recognition algorithms with a database of social microtransactions. The practical upshot of the reward and punishment system is that someone can be denied a rail ticket or admission of children to colleges if the score is low and can enjoy discounted travel fares or lower waiting times at hospitals if the score is high. The policy was lampooned by the British science fiction television series *Black Mirror* in an episode titled *Nosedive*.

Even in democracies, the temptation of the ruling class to usurp more power than what is granted by the constitution remains the biggest threat to civil liberty. J. R. R. Tolkien's magnum opus *The Lord of the Rings* is, among other things, an allegory of how power can corrupt even the noblest of souls. Frodo Baggins was chosen to destroy the One Ring as he was judged by the wise elves and wizards to be the least susceptible to the trappings of power, even more than the judges themselves. Yet Frodo came precariously close to failing his mission. Such is the seduction of power, and why institutions should never be built over perceptions of benevolent despotism. Restricting criticism, planning on behalf of citizens, or watching over the population with millions of security cameras may offer some short-term political gains, but nothing is worth the sacrifice of the spirit and soul of a nation. As Benjamin Franklin once said, *"Those who would give up essential liberty to purchase a little temporary safety deserve neither liberty nor safety."*

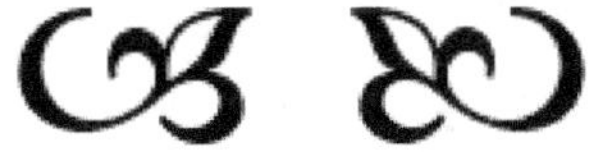

www.ingramcontent.com/pod-product-compliance
Lightning Source LLC
Chambersburg PA
CBHW070046260726
48658CB00002B/749